Damage to top left corner

W9-BOD-805

How Jet Engines Are Made

Text   Julian Moxon
Design   Arthur Lockwood

Contents

Facts On File Publications
New York, New York ● Bicester, England

What is a jet engine?

If you visit a busy airport, have a look at the engines mounted on the aircraft. You will see them hanging under the wings, or fixed to the rear of the fuselage. There may be two, three, or even four engines, depending on the type of airplane. A Boeing 747 jumbo jet, for example, needs four engines – which between them produce enough power to light a medium-sized town.

Once this monster has taken to the air, the jets will be running continuously for ten hours or more. On a ten-hour journey they could burn 50,000 gallons (227,305 litres) of fuel – enough to drive a car around the world sixty times!

So what exactly are jet engines? If you look in at the front of one all you will see is what seems to be a big fan. There is even less to see at the other end, because the cowling around the engine extends for quite a long way beyond the rotating parts inside. From a distance, all you can see is a hole, blackened by exhaust smoke.

The job of a jet engine is to produce a very powerful stream of air which will push the aircraft forward. Huge

A Rolls-Royce RB. 211. Four of these jet engines power a Boeing 747. You can see part of the fan sitting back in the engine cowling shell. The engineer has opened a section of the cowling to inspect the engine before take-off.

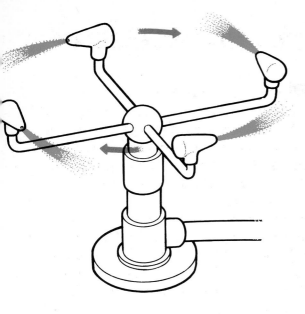

This garden sprinkler is made to spin in the direction of the arrow by the reaction of water escaping from the nozzles. The more water pressure there is, the faster the sprinkler whirls. This same principle of reaction is applied to create the thrust in a jet engine, but instead of water it uses air.

Aircraft are powered either by propeller-driven engines or by jet engines. Propellers push back a large mass of air relatively slowly, while jets force back a smaller mass, but at a much faster rate. Jets therefore work more efficiently on high speed aircraft, while propellers are better suited to slower types.

quantities of air enter at the front, pass through the rotating machinery inside, and are expelled at high speed from the exhaust at the rear. It works something like a garden sprinkler, which spins round when water is forced through the nozzles. This is known as 'jet reaction', because as the water leaves the nozzles it 'reacts' or presses against them. You can test jet reaction yourself by holding the end of a hosepipe and turning on the tap. As soon as the water comes out you will feel a force pushing the hosepipe nozzle towards you.

Instead of water, a jet engine uses air to provide the reaction. But before it can be made to do any work, the air has to be squeezed. The machinery in the engine is therefore designed to squeeze the air as much as possible before letting it escape out of the exhaust. This machinery is known as the **gas turbine**. A jet engine consists of the gas turbine, the casings that surround it, and other equipment, such as the **thrust reverser**, which helps to slow the aircraft down when it lands.

Jet engines were first used to power aircraft about forty years ago, towards the end of the Second World War. Before that, forward thrust was always provided by **propellers**, turned by a **piston engine**. When airplanes first took to the air at the beginning of this century, their engines were little more than copies of those used in cars. But they were soon developed, so that by the 1940s aircraft were reaching speeds of up to 400 mph (644 kmph) – which was as fast as a piston-powered airplane could fly. Then came the jet engine which, fortunately, was invented in time to take over from the piston engine, pushing aircraft to higher speeds than anybody had thought possible. Nowadays, jet-powered aircraft can travel way beyond 400 mph (644 kmph). Concorde, with her four jet engines each providing 28,000 pounds (12,700 kgs) of thrust, can reach 1250 mph (2011 kmph) – which is about twice the speed of sound.

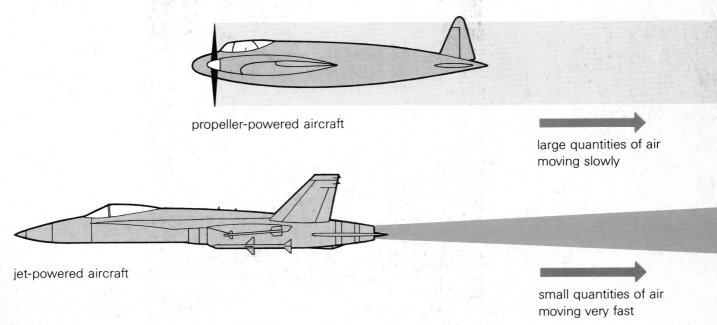

propeller-powered aircraft

large quantities of air moving slowly

jet-powered aircraft

small quantities of air moving very fast

How a jet engine works

The principle of jet propulsion is seen when an inflated balloon is released. The balloon rushes across the room, propelled by the reaction of air rushing from the nozzle. In a jet aircraft the air reacts against the machinery, pushing the engine, and the aircraft, forward.

Inside a jet engine there are hundreds of small blades, like this high-pressure turbine blade. The turbine turns the compressor, which provides the flow of air needed to drive the aircraft forward. Turbine blades sit in an extremely hot jet of gas, produced by the combustor, and have to be designed to withstand the high temperature.

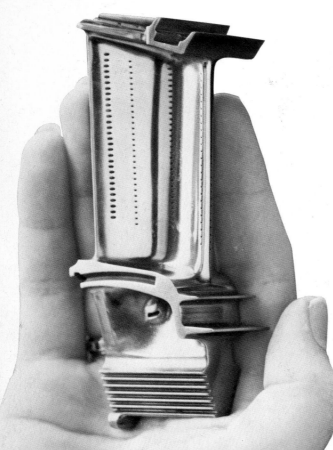

The jet engine's job is to force as much air out of its exhaust duct as possible so that it will be pushed forwards – just as a toy balloon flies across the room when the air rushes out of it.

The way in which a jet engine works is really quite simple. Think of the propeller used to power a toy airplane. Its blades are twisted into curves which direct the air towards the rear of the airplane. The faster the propeller spins, the more air there is flowing back to push the airplane forwards.

Inside a jet engine this pushing job is carried out by a **compressor**, which is really a series of 'propellers', one behind the other, all mounted on the same shaft. But the blades of a compressor are much shorter than those of a propeller, and there are many more of them, as you will see from the picture on page 10. Also, compressors spin round much faster than propellers, pushing enormous quantities of air back along the engine and compressing it as it goes.

Most of the air forced back by the compressor is used to push the aircraft forwards. But some of it is mixed with *fuel*. It then becomes a vapour, which is burned in a **combustion chamber** or **combustor**. This makes it expand very rapidly, and the only escape for it is through an opening in the rear of the combustion chamber. It rushes out of here with tremendous energy, and carries on through the **exhaust duct**. It then joins the air from the compressor and helps to push the aircraft forwards.

Finally there is the **turbine**, which extracts from the gas-stream the power needed to drive the compressor. It behaves just like a windmill which turns when blown by the wind. It is mounted on the same shaft as the compressor, and is blown round by the hot, high-pressure air rushing out of the combustion chamber. The turbine is one of the most difficult parts of a jet engine to make. It has to work for many hours while running in a jet of very hot gases, so it has to be immensely strong, as well as light in weight.

The power of a jet engine is measured in pounds of thrust. This may seem odd, because pounds are usually a measurement of weight, not power – but in fact it makes sense, for when we say that a jet engine produces 20,000 lbs (9072 kgs) of thrust, we mean that it is powerful enough to exert a forward force of 20,000 lbs. For example, when you push a 2 lb bag of sugar along a table you are producing a force of 2 lbs. The engines of big passenger jets can each exert up to 60,000 lbs (27,216 kgs) of thrust, which is about twenty-five times the weight of a family car.

reaction | action

Comparison of jet and piston engines

Jet and piston engines work on a similar principle. Each operates in four stages: intake, compression, combustion, and exhaust. In a jet engine, however, combustion of fuel is continuous, whereas in a piston engine, combustion occurs only once in every revolution.

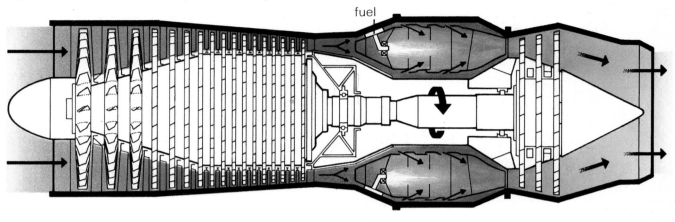

AIR INTAKE	COMPRESSION	COMBUSTION	EXHAUST

Jet Air is sucked into the intake by the compressor.

Jet The compressor pushes air towards the combustor, each row of blades squeezing it a little more.

Jet Air is forced into the combustor, fuel is added, and a continuous torch of burning gases is formed. An igniter starts off the combustion process.

Piston With the piston at the top of its movement, a timed spark ignites the fuel/air mixture. This explodes, forcing the piston down. The piston is connected to the rear wheels via a crankshaft and gearbox.

Jet The hot combustion gases expand through the turbine and into the exhaust duct, pushing the engine forwards. The energy extracted from the exhaust by the turbine is used to drive the compressor.

Piston The piston rises, pushing waste gases out through the open exhaust valve. The gases are discharged through the exhaust pipe.

Piston As the piston travels down, a mixture of air and fuel is drawn through the inlet valve.

Piston With both valves closed, the piston rises, compressing the air as it does so.

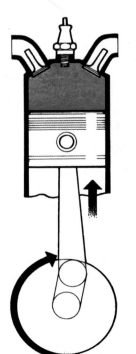 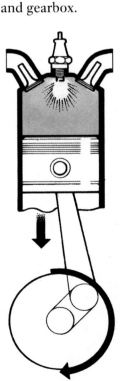 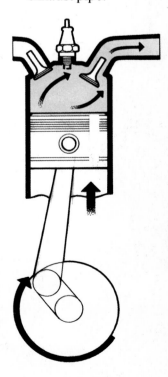

AIR/FUEL INTAKE	COMPRESSION	COMBUSTION	EXHAUST

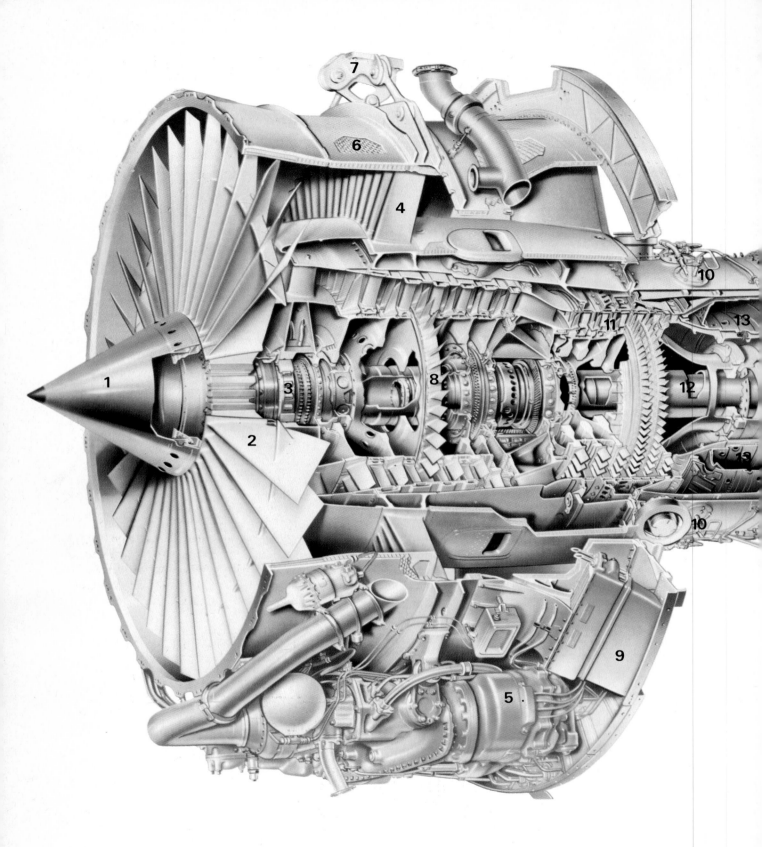

This cutaway drawing shows the Rolls-Royce
RB.211-535 with its main parts identified.

1 Fan spinner
2 Fan
3 Fan support bearing
4 Fan outlet guide-vane
5 Gearbox
6 Noise suppression material
7 Front engine mounting
8 Intermediate-pressure compressor
9 Oil tank
10 Fuel manifold
11 High-pressure compressor
12 Low-pressure and
intermediate-pressure engine shafts
13 Combustion chamber
14 High-pressure turbine
15 Intermediate-pressure turbine
16 Low-pressure turbine
17 Rear engine mounting
18 Discs
19 Rear support vanes
20 Exhaust cone

Inside a jet engine

A jet engine, as you can see in the cutaway drawing, is extremely complex, consisting of around 20,000 parts. This Rolls-Royce RB.211-535 is designed in three sections, with each section mounted on a separate shaft. It is therefore called a three-shaft engine. The **low-pressure** (LP) section consists of the fan and the low-pressure turbine which drives it, while the **intermediate** section comprises the six-stage intermediate-pressure (IP) compressor and IP turbine. The air is finally squeezed in the six-stage **high-pressure** (HP) compressor, which is driven by the HP turbine. After passing through the compressors the air is burned in the combustor before expanding through the turbines and out into the exhaust duct. Three-shaft engines are built only by Rolls-Royce. Jet engines built by other manufacturers have two shafts; in these engines the fan and IP compressor form one unit, which is driven by the LP turbine.

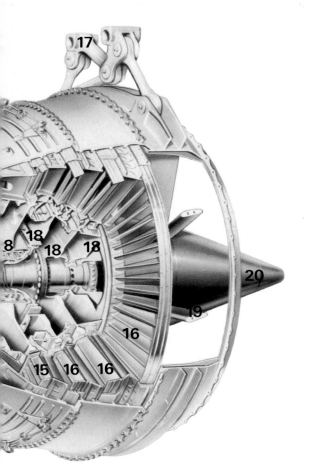

Below is an exploded diagram showing how the engine illustrated on the opposite page is fitted inside the cowling and 'C' ducts. The complete unit is joined to the wing by the pylon (see page 21).

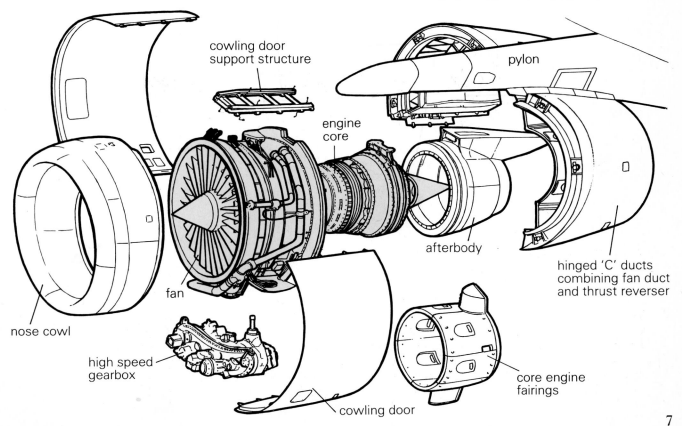

cowling door support structure

pylon

engine core

afterbody

fan

nose cowl

high speed gearbox

cowling door

hinged 'C' ducts combining fan duct and thrust reverser

core engine fairings

Building a jet engine

It takes about two years to build a modern jet engine – longer than it takes to build the aircraft that it will power.

A major jet engine manufacturer employs up to 40,000 people. At least half of them are engineers working on the design and looking after every stage of production and every component, from the smallest compressor blade to the finished engine.

Because a jet engine has to work so hard and because it has to be very reliable, each of its components must be made to an extremely high standard. In the type of engine which powers the Boeing 747 jumbo jets, there are almost 25,000 parts. Each part has to be designed to the highest possible standard by skilled engineers. It can take up to five years to design them all.

Making the parts and then assembling them involves a great deal of planning. Some of the parts may be produced by small engineering or electronics companies operating a long way from the main engine factory. For example, fan blades for American engines are produced by a company who specialise in the different techniques required. Turbine blades for some American engines are made in England, while castings for a British engine may be German-made.

Every single part carries its own number and individual record card. As it passes through the factory all the different processes that it goes through are recorded on the card, so that even the smallest detail of its manufacture is known. If a fault occurs during the engine's life, investigators can check back to the records and find out if the problem was anything to do with the way in which a component was made.

Computers play an increasingly important part in helping engineers to design jet engines. In this illustration the computer has produced a three-dimensional outline of a turbine blade. The operator can view the blade from any angle and ask the computer to print out details of the design, along with all the dimensions needed. Often the computer forms part of a production network which includes robots.

The traditional way of designing jet-engine components is by producing engineering drawings. Several drawings may be needed for each part, which means that for an entire jet engine many thousands have to be created. The engineers in the photograph are discussing the design of a turbine blade. Nowadays drawings are usually produced automatically by computers, working from dimensions supplied by a design engineer. They can be made in a fraction of the time that it took to draw them by hand.

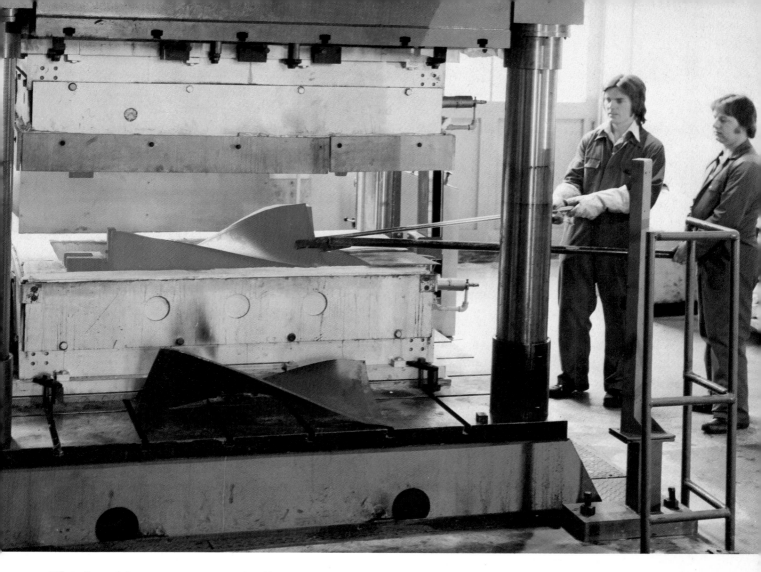

The three biggest companies, Rolls-Royce, Pratt & Whitney and General Electric, have several plants in different locations. Pratt & Whitney, for example, develop their civil engines in Connecticut and their military engines in Florida.

Some engines are produced by the manufacturers of several countries working together. Satellite links make possible the transfer of drawings and information, each manufacturer working on a separate part of the engine.

One such engine is the CFM56, a very successful 22,000 lb turbofan for medium-sized aircraft. The CFM56 fan, and the low-pressure turbine that drives it, are built by the French company Snecma, while the 'heart' of the engine, the high-pressure compressor and turbine, is the responsibility of General Electric in the US.

Complete CFM56s are assembled in both France and the USA. In each case the parts are flown across the Atlantic and carried to their final destination by road. Computers keep track of progress and the information is flashed from one country to another by satellite.

The many parts of the jet engine are tested in different ways by the most advanced equipment. This is ultrasonic testing of a fan blade, to detect flaws in the metal.

Making blades for the big fan at the front of a Rolls-Royce jet engine. Here a titanium blade skin is being removed from a hot press. The skin will be joined to its mate, forming a hollow blade. For strength, the cavity between the skins is filled with a honeycomb core of titanium.

The compressor

A big jet engine gulps down around two and a half thousand tons of air for every hour that it is working – which means that during a 6½-hour flight from London to New York it needs more than seventeen thousand tons of air. All of this air is pumped by **compressors**, which are the 'heart' of a jet engine. They work like big, powerful pumps which thoroughly squeeze the air sucked in through the engine-intake. The more they squeeze the air, the more efficiently the engine will work.

Compressors look rather like porcupines. They have many rows of blades attached to the outside of a drum, which is tapered from front to back. The long blades are at the front, the short ones at the back. Each row of blades turns in the same way as a simple electric fan, and each passes air to the row behind. As the air moves back along the compressor it has less and less space to occupy, because of the tapering (see picture), so it becomes squeezed. A modern jet-engine compressor can squeeze the air into a space about twenty times smaller than the opening at the intake. It is therefore said to have a compression ratio of 20:1.

On most modern jet engines there is an especially big set of blades at the front of the engine. They are mounted on a different shaft from that which turns the main compressor and they operate like a powerful fan, blowing air around the outside of the engine as well as through the compressor itself. The fan improves the engine's performance, particularly during low speeds at take-off and climb.

When the air passing through the compressor has been squeezed, it is burned in the combustor. It then expands very quickly, rushing out of the exhaust in a jet, and helping to push the aircraft forwards.

With so much work to do, compressors have to be very strong. Used in aircraft, they must also be light. To make something strong and light, special materials have to be used (this of course applies to all the components of a jet engine).

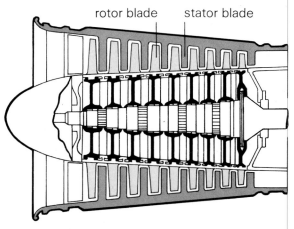

rotor blade   stator blade

A jet engine compressor consists of a *rotor* and a *stator*. The stator blades are attached to the inside of the compressor drum and do not rotate. Air passing through the engine first meets a row of big stator blades, called guide-vanes. These direct the air at the first row of rotor blades.

This is a high-pressure compressor rotor from a modern jet engine, the Pratt & Whitney PW2037. The engine powers the 180-seat Boeing 757, and produces 37,600lbs of thrust. The compressor is made up of 12 stages, each stage consisting of a number of blades. Driven by the high-pressure turbine, it rotates up to 12,000 times a minute. Note how the blades get shorter towards the back of the compressor, where the air is squeezed as tightly as possible before it enters the combustion chamber.

The turbine

Of all the parts of the engine, turbines have the most exacting job to do. As mentioned on page 4, they work on the same principle as a windmill, though a windmill has only a few sails, while turbines needs up to one hundred blades. They are placed in a powerful jet of hot, high-pressure gas which rushes out of the combustion chamber at a temperature of up to 1200°C (2544°F) – hot enough to make the turbines glow red as they spin round. They can make as many as 20,000 revolutions per minute.

Turbines are constructed so that they take enough energy from the hot gas-jet to turn the compressor, which is fixed to the opposite end of the main engine shaft. The rest of the energy in the gas-jet passes out of the exhaust and is used to push the aircraft forwards.

The blades of a turbine are fixed to a large wheel, or **disc**, in such a way that they can be removed separately for repair. A row of blades is called a **stage**. There is nearly always more than one stage. In big jet engines up to seven turbine stages may be used. They are usually divided into two sections – the **high-pressure turbine** and the **low-pressure turbine**. The high-pressure turbine – consisting of the two stages nearest to the combustor – uses the energy which it extracts from the exhaust jet to drive the high-pressure part of the compressor. The low-pressure turbine – which is connected to a shaft passing through the centre of the engine – drives the low-pressure compressor. This compressor is the part which often has a big fan at the front of it.

The low-pressure turbine may also be used for other jobs. For example, on jet engines which power helicopters it would be joined to a shaft which turns the rotor. It can also be used for turning aircraft propellers or ships' screws.

A low-pressure turbine. This extracts enough energy from the hot gases rushing through the engine to drive the big fan at the front. There are five stages, and you can see that the blades have rings around the outside. The rings are designed to prevent the gases escaping as they pass through the turbine into the exhaust duct. The turbine blades are attached to discs, fixed to the shaft in the centre.

How compressor and turbine discs are made

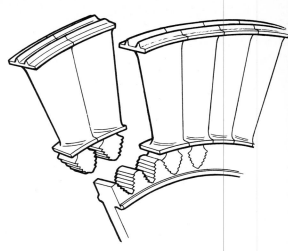

If you tie a small piece of wood to the end of a length of string and whirl it round your head, you will feel the wood pulling away from you, even if you whirl it quite slowly. The same force acts on the blades of compressors and turbines spinning at some 20,000 revolutions per minute: but because they spin so fast, the pull is much bigger. In fact, the force wrenching at the blades on their mountings can at full power reach *several tons*. To stand up to this force, the blade mountings, or roots, have to be extremely strong, and very carefully made.

The disc to which the compressor and turbine blades of all large jet engines are fixed looks like a big wheel with teeth. As it has to carry the load of all the blades pulling away at once, it is a heavy, solid structure. It must never break, for if it did it would cause enormous damage to the engine.

When discs are made, they must be as perfect as possible. The smallest crack or imperfection in the metal can become the starting place for a fracture, which will grow as the disc spins. They must also be light, since they make up most of the weight of a jet engine.

The traditional method of making compressor and turbine discs is by *forging* the metal into shape. First a large block of metal is roughly cut, or *machined*, to size, then it is heated until very hot, and stamped into the right shape. Heating the metal not only makes it softer and easier to force into shape, but also helps to remove faults which could lead to cracks.

The latest method of manufacturing turbine and compressor discs ensures that the metal is almost completely free from imperfections. It is called 'powder metallurgy' and is now being used in the manufacture of some jet engines. In order to produce discs by this method, a very fine powder is made by pouring molten metal on to a fast-spinning turn-table. When the molten metal hits the surface, it breaks into millions of fine droplets which are flung from the edge of the table. The moment they leave the table, the droplets cool and solidify, forming a very fine metal powder. The cooling process happens extremely quickly, with the temperature dropping by about 1000°C (2120°F) in half a second. During this half-second the molecules within the metal powder are 'frozen' in their positions so quickly that the metal does not have time to pick up impurities.

The roots of a turbine or compressor blade are shaped so that they lock into the 'teeth' of the disc which carries them. Most jet engines use the arrangement shown in the diagram above. Because of its shape this is known as a 'fir tree' root. The blades are slotted into place around the disc and secured with a bolt. They are free to rock slightly in their mountings, to help spread the enormous load which each root carries.

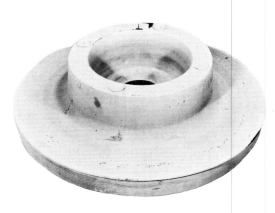

This is what a disc looks like before it is finally shaped. The example here is from a high-pressure turbine. It has been pressed into shape by forging. The metal is as near perfect as possible, to ensure maximum strength. After forging, the disc is mounted on to a giant cutting machine and cut automatically to exactly the correct dimensions for the engine: within a few thousandths of an inch.

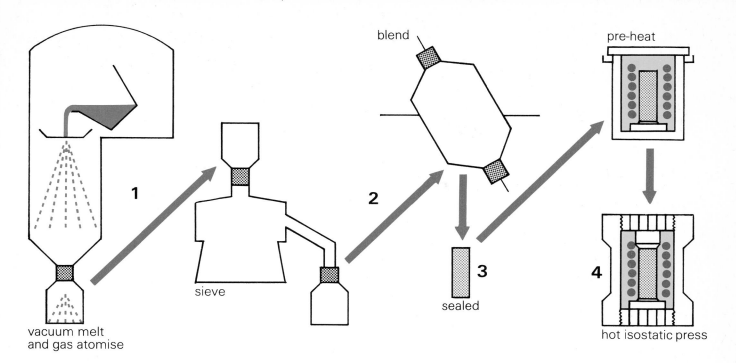

1 vacuum melt and gas atomise

sieve

2 blend

3 sealed

pre-heat

4 hot isostatic press

Next, the powder is compressed, under hundreds of tons of pressure, into a shape very similar to that of the turbine or compressor disc. To make the disc ready for the engine, only a small amount of tidying up needs to be done on a large cutting machine: a process which is quick and inexpensive.

The forged disc is then machined again; the roots that will carry the blades are cut; and the finished product is despatched to be carefully inspected.

Today, much of the manufacturing work is controlled by computers. They help to design the disc, making all the calculations needed to ensure that it is as strong and as light as possible. They also control the machines which do the cutting.

Making powdered metal turbine discs. A forming case is filled with metal powder made by the process described at the end of page 12, and put into a vacuum (1). The case is vibrated, so that the powder when shaken down becomes tightly packed (2). The vacuum ensures that there are no air 'voids' within. Next the case is sealed (3) and the metal powder is subjected to extremely high pressure – about 25,000 pounds per square inch (4). It is also heated, so that the metal particles become fused together, forming the disc, which can then be removed from the forming case and machined to its final shape.

Hard-facing a high-pressure turbine disc. The disc teeth need to have a very hard surface to cope with the wear and tear of carrying turbine blades. The operator watches the spraying of a special metal on to the spinning turbine disc. Under intensive heat the hard-facing metal fuses with that of the disc.

How compressor and turbine blades are made

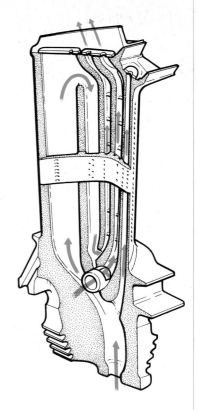

One of the ways most frequently used for manufacturing the blades of modern compressors and turbines is by *casting*: a method first used by the Chinese about 2000 years ago for making statues. You can think of casting as being something like making a jelly in a mould. The liquid is poured into it, cools, and sets to the shape of the mould.

Before it is cast, the metal has to be heated up to a very high temperature so that it melts. It can then be poured into the *mould*, which is the shape of the compressor or turbine blades. Generally, several different types of metal are mixed together, forming what is called an *alloy*.

The moulds are made of a ceramic material, similar to that used for making cups and saucers. The molten mixture is poured into the moulds in a casting furnace, and allowed to cool. The ceramic is then broken away, revealing the freshly cast blades. These are then cut to their final shape by very accurate cutting machines. After the blades have been made, they are all carefully tested.

Compressor blades have to withstand the powerful pressure from the enormous quantities of air pumped back down the engine. They also have to withstand damage caused by objects sucked in at the intake. So they must be tough. They must also be light in weight; and they become very hot, particularly at the end nearest to the combustor, where the pressure is highest. The alloy used for these blades, therefore, is one which gives them the best combination of strength and lightness.

Turbine blades are cast in a different way from compressor blades. If you take a piece of balsa wood like that used in a model aircraft, and try to break it, you will find that it is stronger in one direction than it is in the other. This is because the wood has a 'grain'. With turbine blades, the grain in the metal is made to lie in the correct direction, which is along the blade. This is achieved while the blade cools after it has been cast. The process is called *directional solidifying*.

For turbines, special alloys have been developed so that they can cope with temperatures of up to 1300°C. They are based on nickel, and have small amounts of aluminium, titanium, and other metals designed to retain the blade's strength while it is in operation.

To reduce the enormous heat created by the gas-jets, the turbine blades are cooled by air passing through a maze of tiny holes within them. The holes, or *cooling passages*, are arranged so that the blades are cooled in exactly the right places. You can see the passages in the picture. Cooling enables the blades to operate in gas streams hotter than the melting point of the metal from which they are made.

Jet engine turbine blades work at very high temperatures, sometimes becoming red hot. They usually have to be cooled by air blown via the compressor into the root of each blade. The network of cooling passages within the blade, which is very complex, ensures that the blade skin is prevented from burning. The inner passages are formed during the casting process. The hundreds of tiny holes connecting the passages to the blade surface are drilled either by a small laser beam, or by spark erosion. This is a technique that uses a carefully controlled spark to eat away the metal.

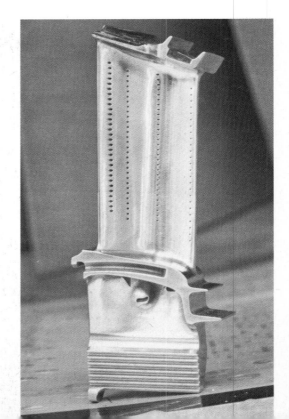

Making turbine blades using the 'lost wax' process. Wax copies of the blade are created by pouring wax into a metal mould; allowing it to set; and removing the mould. The wax blades are then mounted on a 'tree' to form a cluster. The cluster in the picture contains eight wax turbine blades, ready for dipping into a ceramic slurry.

A cluster of wax blades being removed from the ceramic slurry. The blades are dipped into the slurry several times, building up a ceramic coating about ¼-inch thick. Next, the cluster is heated to a temperature of about 1000°C, which hardens the ceramic coat and melts the wax. Molten metal is then poured into the ceramic shell and allowed to harden in special ovens. The ceramic coat is broken away, leaving the turbine blade, which is now ready to be accurately machined to its final shape.

The turbine blade is hardened under very carefully controlled conditions. This is an automatic, computer-controlled oven for making directionally solidified blades.

Fuel control and the combustion chamber

Before they can do any work, all engines need fuel. Jet engines burn a type of fuel which is very similar to paraffin. It is called Jet-A. On a long flight lasting seven or eight hours, the four engines of a jumbo jet will gulp down 30,000 gallons (136,383 litres) of it.

The Jet-A is stored in the wings of the aircraft and is fed to the engines by high-speed pumps. When it reaches the engines it passes through a **fuel control system** which accurately monitors the fuel before pumping it into the combustion chamber, where it is burned, releasing its energy to drive the turbines and to push the aircraft forwards.

Before the fuel can burn it has to be mixed with exactly the right quantity of air. This also applies to a car engine, which uses a carburetor to do the mixing. In a jet engine the mixing is carried out in the combustion chamber. If the mixture is to be completely burned, about fifteen times more air than fuel is needed. Extra air, not needed for burning fuel, passes around the combustor to prevent it from overheating.

The job of the fuel control system is to make sure that the correct amount of fuel is pumped into the combustion chamber throughout an aircraft's flight – from engine starting, through full power take-off, to cruise. In order to do this, it has to know how much air is passing through the engine, so that it can adjust the mixture correctly.

The amount of air needed by the engine changes constantly, depending on the aircraft's speed and height, and on the outside temperature. (The density of air at 30,000 feet, 9,144 metres, is much lower than it is on the ground.) So a fuel control system is very complicated. It is a kind of 'brain' which constantly looks after the fuel needs of the engine. Its **sensors** (devices which 'sense out') measure air pressure and temperature, and a number of other factors, such as engine speed.

On some very up-to-date jet engines the 'thinking' is done by a computer, which makes life easier for pilots, flight engineers and maintenance men.

When the fuel reaches the combustion chamber it is forced under great pressure through very small nozzles which break the liquid into tiny droplets. It then mixes more easily with the air which rushes through the combustion chamber.

The **combustion chamber**, as you can see from the picture, is wrapped around the middle of the engine, between the compressor and the turbines. The compressor, as described on page 10, pumps a lot of air back down the engine. Some of the air is channelled into the combustion

Right The combustion chamber, or combustor, is responsible for converting the fuel energy into power to make the turbines spin. Fuel and air are sprayed through nozzles, at very high pressure, into the chamber. The mixture is ignited, forming a continuous flame which rushes backwards. More air is introduced through holes in the side of the combustion chamber to prevent the walls from becoming too hot, and from burning. The escaping gases are directed at the turbine by the nozzle guide-vanes.

Left A partly assembled combustion chamber. The fuel spray nozzles will fit into the large holes in the rear. The holes in the walls are for cooling.

chamber, where it is thoroughly mixed with the fuel droplets before being burned.

You can think of the combustion chamber as a kind of blow torch, which when the fuel is burned produces enough heat to warm 17,000 standard-size, eight-room domestic dwellings. During the burning process the mixture of fuel and air expands very rapidly and is forced under enormous pressure out of the chamber. The gas-jet is aimed at the turbines, blowing them round so that they can turn the fan and compressors which push the aircraft forwards.

Combustion chambers have to mix the air and fuel thoroughly in a very short distance, so they are a complicated shape. And since they work for many hours at high temperatures they have to be made of very special metals. Sometimes a metal called *titanium* is used. This comes from an ore found in certain rocks. It is a very hard substance, and as it is difficult to mould into the right shapes it is only used in aircraft when there is a particularly tough job to do.

Combustion chambers are produced in several sections, which are welded together before they are mounted on the engine. The sections are made by heating up the titanium until it is soft. It is then pushed into a mould under great pressure.

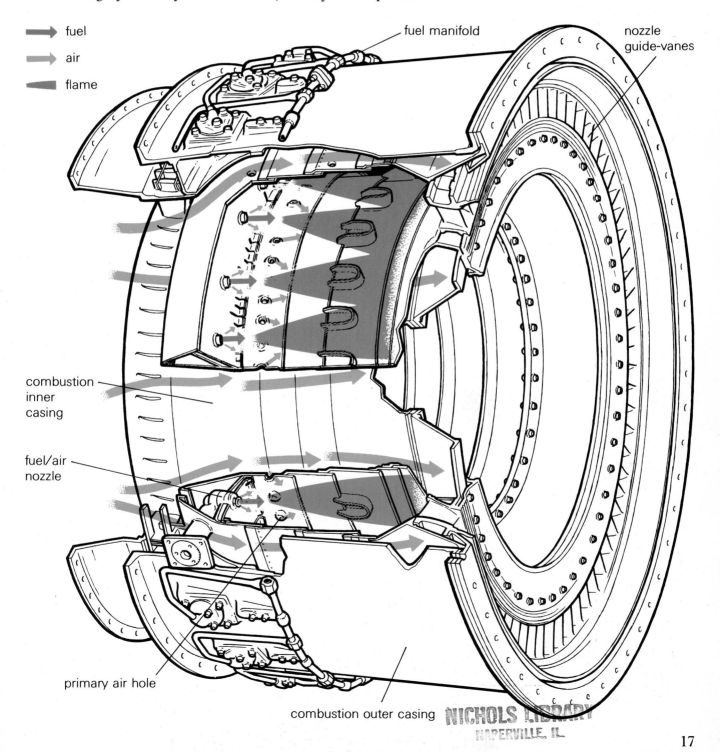

fuel

air

flame

fuel manifold

nozzle guide-vanes

combustion inner casing

fuel/air nozzle

primary air hole

combustion outer casing

17

A modern fighter engine in full reheat. This is the 23,000lb-thrust Pratt & Whitney F100 which powers F-15s and F-16s. Fuel is being pumped into the exhaust system and ignited, greatly increasing the thrust of the engine. The nozzle at the rear is wide open. When reheat is reduced, or switched off, the nozzle contracts, reducing the duct area.

This is an experimental system for reducing the noise made by a civil jet-engine exhaust. The serrated ring is designed to mix the high-speed air – which is produced in the core – with the slower air pushed back by the fan. The slower the final exhaust jet, the less noise it makes. You can test this yourself by blowing through various sizes of tube.

The exhaust system

The exhaust is one of the few systems of a jet engine that you can actually see in action. Its job is to pass the gases rushing through the engine out into the atmosphere. Without it, the engine would perform very badly. By getting the shape of the exhaust duct right, the designers can improve the performance of the rest of the engine.

Aircraft flying at less than the speed of sound need exhaust systems with nozzles that are tapered towards the end. Aircraft flying beyond the speed of sound need nozzles which open out at the end, but which at slower speeds can be tapered.

When you are next at an airport, look at any passenger aircraft, and you will see that the engines are housed in **nacelles** which become narrower towards the rear end. These nacelles form the wall of the **outer exhaust duct**, which carries the air pushed back by the big fan at the front of the engine. The **inner exhaust duct**, which is narrower and extends beyond the outer duct, carries the air pumped back by the **core**, or heart, of the engine.

Between the outer and inner exhaust ducts is the **thrust reverser**, the mechanism which blocks off the air driven back by the fan, thus forcing it in the opposite direction. On landing, the reverse thrust acts as an extra brake and helps to slow the aircraft down.

When you are landing in a passenger aircraft you can hear the increase in engine noise as the wheels touch the ground. This is the moment when the pilot selects reverse thrust, opening the throttle to full power to slow the aircraft down in as short a time as possible.

Aircraft such as Concorde and jet fighters are equipped with adjustable nozzles which are automatically tapered at low speeds, and opened out when maximum power is needed for take-off and supersonic flight. The nozzles are also fitted with **afterburners**, which are used to increase the power of the engine for take-off, climb, and supersonic

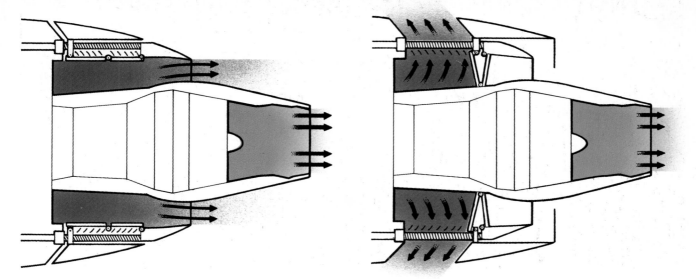

flight. In military aircraft, they are also switched on for combat, when the extra power is sometimes needed to outfly the enemy. If you are at an air show watching a jet fighter taking off, look carefully at the exhaust as the pilot begins his take-off run. You should see the nozzle open out at the end, and a red glow as the afterburner lights up. All modern supersonic aircraft are equipped with afterburners.

The afterburner is a simple mechanism which consists of a ring of fuel nozzles set into the exhaust duct, just behind the turbines. Air from the turbines rushes through the nozzles, is mixed with the fuel, and ignited, turning the exhaust duct into a kind of very powerful blow torch. By means of the afterburner, engine power can be doubled. It can only be used for short periods, because it gulps down a great deal of fuel, but it is a very practical way of increasing power without having to make the engine bigger. For the engines of high speed aircraft, which must be as slim as possible, this is very important.

The exhaust systems of jet engines create enormous heat, particularly if an afterburner is fitted, when the temperature at the nozzle can reach 1500°C (3180°F). This is hot enough to melt most metals, but not titanium, which is therefore often used for parts of the exhaust system which have to withstand great heat, such as the nozzle.

At present, exhaust systems on passenger aircraft are manufactured from aluminium alloy, and lined with special material designed to absorb the noise made by the engine's exhaust jet and its rotating parts.

Some of the latest engines use *composites* for the outer parts of the exhaust duct and engine nacelle. Composites consist of man-made fibres held together by resin. A very successful composite material is Fibreglass, which has many everyday uses. Even lighter and stronger than Fibreglass is Kevlar, which is now being used to build complete light aircraft. As it is so strong it is also used to surround the big fan at the front of the engine to prevent broken blades from escaping through the nacelle.

Reversing the thrust of a jet engine helps to slow the aircraft after touchdown. Only the air of the fan (shown blue) is reversed, since this provides most of the engine's thrust. Large doors block the fan duct, forcing the air to escape through a grille in the outer casing. The grille is angled so that it directs the escaping air forwards.

Sound-absorbing acoustic panels like this are used in civil jet engines to reduce fan noise. The tips of a fan blade can exceed the speed of sound, making them one of the noisiest parts of a modern turbofan. The acoustic panels are made of a special lightweight material which is wrapped around the inside of the fan duct.

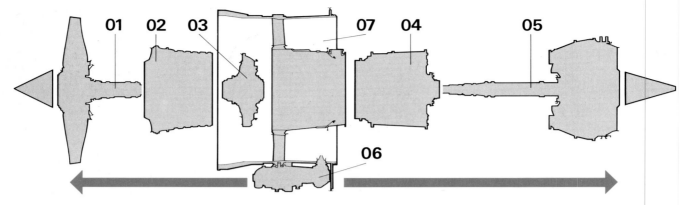

This Rolls-Royce 535 engine consists of seven modules. Each module is a pre-balanced unit, and can be replaced with a new or repaired unit without the necessity of matching it to the rest of the engine.

01 Fan
02 Intermediate-pressure compressor
03 I P module
04 High-pressure system (comprising HP compressor, combustor and HP turbine)
05 Intermediate- and low-pressure turbine
06 Gearbox
07 Fan casing

Assembly

When inspection of the components is complete, assembly of the engine can begin. Most engines today are built from 'modules'; you can think of them as building blocks. Rolls-Royce's biggest range of passenger engines, the RB.211 series, consists of up to eleven modules, or blocks. Smaller engines are likely to have fewer.

A module is a working section of the engine, such as a high-pressure turbine, a compressor or a combustion chamber. Each module is constructed in a different part of the factory – or by another company. When the modules are ready they are taken to the part of the factory where engines are assembled. They are then checked and slotted into place, which is a fairly simple operation. The engine is either built vertically or horizontally in a big gantry which can turn the engine over so that work can be carried out on both sides.

When all the modules have been bolted together the supporting components (known as the 'peripherals') such as oil and hydraulic pipes, generators and electrical wiring, are then added, and the engine is ready for testing.

Once it has been proved that the engine can meet all the requirements, it is transported to the aircraft manufacturer, either by air – in a big cargo plane – or by ship. Low-loading lorries then carry the engine to the aircraft factory. As it is worth at least two million dollars and weighs up to six tonnes it must be handled very carefully.

Engines are attached to the aircraft's wings by means of pylons, which are designed to carry the weight of the engines and to transfer their thrust to the airframe. Fuel passes through the pylons to the engines from tanks in the wing, while electrical and hydraulic power is transferred by wires and pipes through the pylons to the aircraft.

If you watch an aircraft as it taxies along the runway you will notice that the engines are 'nodding'. They must be allowed to swing slightly – otherwise their weight would be too heavy for the wing to bear. The pylon is designed to allow the engine to 'nod' while holding it firmly in place.

Installing the fan on a big jet engine, the Rolls-Royce RB.211. The fan is one of the 'modules' of the engine.

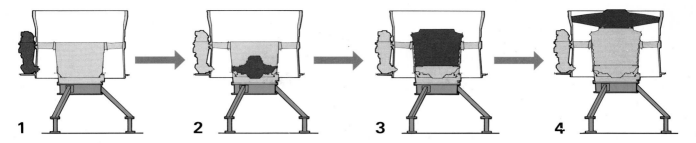

Module build

Stage 1 The fancase module 07 is bolted to a specially designed table called a *build-stool*, and the gearbox 06 is attached.

Stage 2 Module 03 is lowered into the fancase and secured.

Stage 3 Intermediate-pressure compressor module 02 is added.
Stage 4 Fan module 01 is attached.

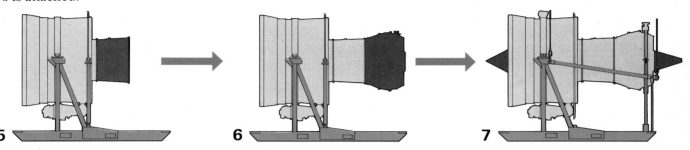

Stage 5 The engine is now placed in a horizontal build-stand, and the high-pressure system module 04 is bolted on.

Stage 6 The intermediate and low-pressure turbine module is joined to module 04.

Stage 7 The exhaust cone and fan spinner are attached, and the engine is made ready for despatch.

The big jet engines which power aircraft such as the Boeing 747 are joined to the wing by pylons, which also carry fuel lines; hydraulic and electrical services; and control-cables. Pylons have a very demanding job, and are manufactured from solid metal for maximum strength. But they must be designed to allow the engine to 'nod' to relieve stress on the wing when the aircraft is flying through turbulence or taxiing along the runway.

Looking at a big turbofan from the rear. This engine, which is being tested, is already attached to its pylon. The big 'C'-shaped doors (or ducts) are opened to give access to the core.

These engines are being fitted with electrical wiring looms, and hydraulic pipework. They are mounted vertically, with the fan module uppermost. Cleanliness is essential in a jet engine factory. Floors are polished, and small components are kept in sealed plastic bags until needed.

Fitting the 'hot section' of the engine, comprising the turbines and combustor, to the fan and compressor section.

A row of almost complete engines at Rolls-Royce's factory in Derby. You can see the two location points at which the engines are attached to their pylons, on top of the casing at either end. These RB 211-535s will power the Boeing 757, a new 180-seat airliner.

Made by automation

All the parts of a jet engine are produced to a very high accuracy and must fit together perfectly if they are to be reliable, safe and long-lasting. Only very skilled workmen with many years' experience can operate the machines which cut the metal parts to shape. Today, some of the work is already being carried out by computers, which soon will be involved in every stage of jet engine manufacture, from the original selection of the metal to the final shaping of the parts. Computers are even helping out with the actual design of the engine. They have huge memories which can store all of the information needed to work out the best shape for a particular part. They can then 'draw' the part on a special television screen. The computer can also turn the drawing so that the designer is able to look at it from any angle. All of the dimensions needed to enable it to be cut to shape (engineers call it 'machining') are added automatically.

On the factory floor, robots take care of many of the operations which were previously carried out by skilled men. The robots are not like the ones in science fiction films. You can see a typical one used in a jet engine factory in the photograph above. It is performing a welding operation which would normally take a man around four hours to complete. The robot will do the job in one hour,

A composite photograph showing a robot-controlled welding tip in three different positions. Flux is metered precisely through the needle and deposited on the compressor drum as it rotates.

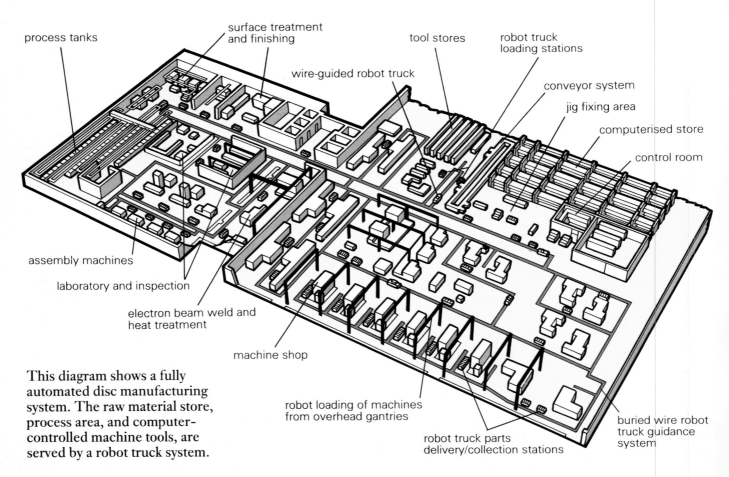

process tanks

surface treatment and finishing

tool stores

robot truck loading stations

wire-guided robot truck

conveyor system

jig fixing area

computerised store

control room

assembly machines

laboratory and inspection

electron beam weld and heat treatment

machine shop

robot loading of machines from overhead gantries

robot truck parts delivery/collection stations

buried wire robot truck guidance system

This diagram shows a fully automated disc manufacturing system. The raw material store, process area, and computer-controlled machine tools, are served by a robot truck system.

and can then proceed to the next job immediately.

There are many other advantages in giving jobs like this to robots. To begin with, they don't mind being put into an unpleasant place to work. Sparks, heat, and dangerous chemicals are no problem: the robot simply goes on working, accurately and quickly. Robots are also very strong, and can make light work of carrying heavy castings, such as turbine discs, from one machine to another, ready for the next operation to be carried out.

Of course, robots have to be told what to do, and the most common technique is to feed into them a special paper tape with a series of holes punched through it. The robot can 'read' the information on the tape by noting the position of the holes, which correspond to the exact requirements of the engineer who designed the part. The tape can be used again and again to instruct any robots in the factory which are free to carry out a particular job.

In jet engine factories of the future, punched tapes will not be necessary. Instead, all of the robot cutting machines will be connected directly to one big computer, which will carry the information needed to instruct the machines to cut the shapes that the designer wants. So when an engine is being built, the computer will know when each machine is ready for its particular job. It will then automatically order the materials from stock and will distribute them to the machines. By the use of these methods jet engines will be built in a much shorter time than they are today, which will make them less expensive.

An automatic robot production line for putting the finishing touches to turbine blades. There are eight pairs of machines in this production line. Each pair, or 'cell', is served by a single robot. At the bottom of the picture you can see a queue of blades waiting to be picked up for work to be carried out. The robot will pick up each one and place it in the machine. While one blade is being trimmed another will be removed from the opposite machine and replaced on the conveyor belt. It will then be carried to the next cell.

Performance testing

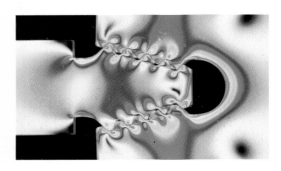

Checking the quality of the alloy in a turbine blade. The TV screen shows a microscope's view of the metal, so that the scientist can look for imperfections.

Scientists use light to make sure that the size and shape of a component are within the correct dimensions. The technique is called *holography*. It uses the interference between two beams of light, one of which is reflected off the object being checked, to produce these patterns. The patterns can be deciphered by skilled engineers.

Wrapping a Kevlar bandage around the fan casing of a big jet engine. The bandage prevents the possibility of a broken fan blade escaping through the casing. Kevlar is an extremely tough, light material, and its use saves 200lbs (91kgs) in weight over the traditional metal containment ring.

The safety of the passengers in an aircraft depends on the reliability of the engines, particularly at take-off, when the engines are all operating at full power and when every component is working under full pressure. Before an engine manufacturing company can sell its engines it must therefore prove to the airlines, aircraft builders, and safety authorities that they are reliable and safe. When this has been proved to the satisfaction of everyone concerned, the engine is given its 'ticket' (certificate of airworthiness) and is allowed to go into service.

An engine is not considered airworthy until all the parts from which it is made have passed tests which prove that their design meets the official requirements. One of the most important of these tests concerns the big fan at the front of the engine.

When an aircraft is accelerating down the runway for take-off, the fan provides about three quarters of the total power produced by the engine. It spins round 6000 times per minute, during which time the fan blades are under enormous strain. At take-off, there is a danger that the engine might suck in an object, such as a bird, just when the aircraft needs all its power. The first components that the object will encounter are the spinning fan blades, so they must be extremely strong in order not to break.

The way in which a fan is tested is by simulating the conditions that are likely to prevail when it is working at full power on the aircraft. So it is mounted in a special frame, and turned by a motor at full speed. Dead birds weighing up to 4 lbs (1.8 kgs) are then fired at the engine from a special 'gun'. The fan must be able to withstand the

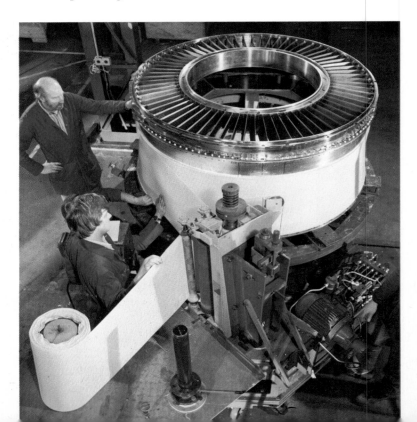

impact of the largest bird without failing in a way that would endanger the aircraft and passengers in flight. This is quite an achievement, since the bird and the fan meet at a combined speed of over 1000 miles (1609 km) per hour.

In order to test the ability of the fan casing to retain a broken fan blade, a blade is deliberately detached at its root by an explosive charge while the fan is running at full power. To achieve this, engineers place an explosive bolt at the root of one of the blades, and detonate it at precisely the correct moment, causing the blade to fly off with tremendous energy. The casing is wrapped in Kevlar to withstand the shock.

This is just one of the many tests that have to be carried out on various components of the engine to prove their safe and efficient performance. When each of the separate components has been tested, the entire engine then has to prove its performance in a **test cell**. There are several test cells in a factory, each specially designed for the different engines that the company makes. Some of them are huge, so that they can deal with the most powerful engines.

The engines are mounted on a gantry. They are then connected to a fuel supply and wired up so that measurements can be taken of the thrust, fuel consumption, and all the other functions that must be tested. Test engineers watch the engine through a thick glass window in the wall of the test cell, or on a TV screen.

Jet engines are also tested in a special chamber which simulates the low-pressure conditions outside an aircraft when it is flying at high altitude.

Once the engineers are satisfied that the engine is safe to fly, it is often mounted on a specially converted aircraft for testing in flight. This will finally prove that it is fit to meet the needs of the airlines that are interested in buying it.

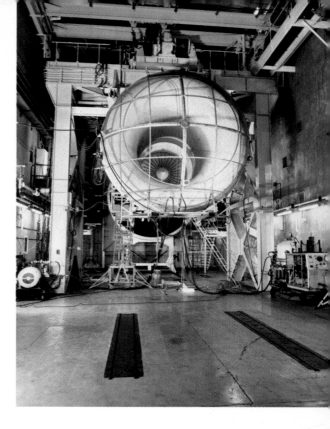

An engine mounted in a test cell. The fan is visible at the end of the inlet duct. The duct is carefully shaped so that engineers can calculate the amount of air used by the engine. The engine (while it is running) is closely monitored by hundreds of electronic probes and watched by TV cameras.

An outdoor test stand. This 50,000lb-thrust General Electric CF6-50 jet engine is being tested for endurance. It will be run for many hours to ensure that it is reliable enough for long-distance flight.

All kinds of jet engines

The Harrier's Pegasus engines have nozzles which can be rotated, enabling the plane to take off vertically, and then fly horizontally like a normal aircraft.

Jet engines are built in many shapes and sizes. The smallest are about the size of a standard loaf of bread, and are used to power long-range missiles and light target aircraft. The biggest and most powerful are the turbofans used on 'wide-bodied' aircraft such as the Boeing 747 jumbo jet. They weigh up to six tonnes.

As well as powering aircraft, jet engines are used for many other purposes – such as on certain naval vessels. For example, a standard A-class Royal Navy destroyer has four gas turbines. Two of them are similar to those fitted to Concorde and are switched on for high-speed dash and manoeuvring. The other two are smaller, and are used for cruising.

In remote parts of the world, gas turbines are used for driving generators to provide electricity. Sometimes they

This racing car, named 'Project Thrust', is powered by a jet engine from a fighter aircraft. 'Thrust' was the first vehicle to break the sound barrier on land.

Top The Pegasus engine seen from above, with nozzles pointing to the rear. *Below* Side view, showing the nozzles rotated to direct air downwards to enable vertical take-off.

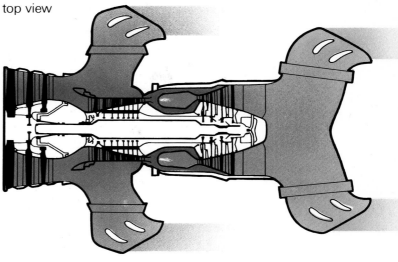

top view

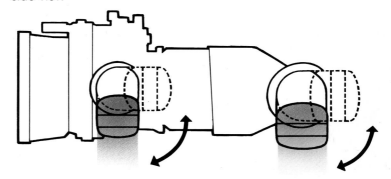

side view

Jet engines for helicopters are very small. In this twin-engined Dauphin helicopter, made by Aérospatiale of France, the engines are mounted side by side just behind the rotor.

are used at normal coal or oil-burning stations as back-up during a breakdown or during maintenance, or to provide peak-load power.

One of the most unusual jet engines in use today is the Rolls-Royce Pegasus, developed specially for the Harrier, the only single-engined vertical take-off fighter in the world. This amazingly versatile aircraft, now used by the US Marines, often puts in an appearance at air shows, when it demonstrates its ability to hover, fly backwards and sideways, and to take off and land vertically.

From the diagram on this page you can see that the Pegasus engine is equipped with four nozzles – two at the front and two at the rear. The rear nozzles take hot air from the exhaust. The front nozzles are fed by cool air from the fan. In a normal engine the fan would pass this air back along the nacelle to provide only forward thrust. But for vertical take-off the Harrier also needs downward thrust. So the air from the fan and the exhaust is passed through rotatable nozzles which can be pointed both downwards and backwards.

At present the Harrier cannot fly beyond the speed of sound, but engineers are experimenting on a new and more powerful version of Pegasus, equipped with specially designed burners which are placed in the front nozzles and which considerably increase the speed of the air passing through them. If the experiment is successful the modified Harrier will be able to fly at almost 1000 miles per hour (1609 kmph).

Glossary

Afterburner A device which doubles the power of a fighter engine. Fuel is sprayed into the exhaust duct and mixed with the hot air blown back by the engine. It is then ignited, producing a powerful 'blow torch' which rushes out of the nozzle at the rear of the exhaust.

Alloy When two or more metals are mixed, the mixture is called an alloy. Alloys produce not only the best properties of each metal used but sometimes they also have extra strength or flexibility.

Carburetor A device used on piston engines to mix fuel and air in exactly the right amounts before it is drawn into the engine for ignition.

Casting A metal object produced by pouring molten metal into a mould, where it cools and sets into the required shape.

Combustion chamber/Combustor The part of a jet engine where high-pressure air from the compressor is mixed with fuel, and burned.

Compressor The 'heart' of the jet engine. A series of spinning blades which suck air in through the inlet, compressing it as much as possible. The high-pressure air is passed on to the combustion chamber for burning.

Core The high-pressure (HP) section of the engine, consisting of the HP compressor, the combustion chamber and HP turbine.

Cowling The smooth metal shroud which surrounds the engine.

Disc Each row of rotating blades in a jet engine is attached to the rim of a disc. The disc has slotted 'teeth', which grip the blades firmly as it spins.

Exhaust pipe The 'tube' at the rear of the engine into which the jet of hot air is discharged. The air is channelled through the duct to the atmosphere.

Gantry A large metal structure to which jet engines are bolted for testing.

Generator A device which produces electrical power for the aircraft. It is driven from the engine by gears.

Igniter Used to ignite the mixture of fuel and compressed air when it first enters the combustion chamber.

Module A section of engine comprising many components. It can be removed as one piece. A jet engine is built up from several modules, usually six to eleven.

Nacelle Another term for cowling.

Nozzle The device at the rear end of the exhaust duct through which the jet travels before meeting the atmosphere. Fighter engines often have nozzles which can be automatically varied in size to make them perform more efficiently.

Powder metallurgy A way of producing near-perfect metal components. Metal powder is compressed under very high pressure into a shape close to that of the finished item.

Pylon The metal structure connecting the engine to the wing, or to the fuselage.

Root The part of a compressor or turbine blade which keeps it attached to the disc.

Stage Each row of blades in a jet engine is called a stage. A typical compressor, for example, might have ten stages.

Subsonic Below the speed of sound, which is 762mph (1226kmph) at sea-level.

Supersonic Above the speed of sound.

Thrust reverser A device which reverses the flow of air to help slow the aircraft down when landing.

Turbine The machine which drives the compressor. It is made to spin by hot gases rushing from the combustor.

Turbofan A type of jet engine in which the core drives a fan at the front. The fan helps the engine to be more efficient at slower speeds.

Facts and figures

Fastest military jet aircraft
Mikoyan Mig-25 'Foxbat' Mach 3.2;
2,110mph/3,394kmph. (USSR).

Most powerful passenger jet engine
GE CF6-80C2, run at over 62,000lb/28,180kg thrust in 1983. (USA).

Most powerful military jet engine
Tumanski turbojet powering Mig-25 'Foxbat'.
Thrust 30,864lb/14,000kg. (USSR).

Fastest passenger jet aircraft
BAe/Aérospatiale Concorde. Cruising speed is Mach 2.2; 1,450mph/2330kmph. (UK/France).

Biggest production jet engine
General Electric TF39 powering Lockheed C-5A Galaxy military airlifter. (USA).
Diameter 8.3ft (2.54 metres).
Length 15.7ft (4.7 metres).
Thrust 41,100lb/18,680kg.

Smallest production jet engine
Williams WR2-6 turbojet powering small target aircraft. (USA).
Diameter 10.8in (274mm).
Length 22.3in (522mm).
Thrust 125lb/57kg.

World's only production vertical take-off and landing engine
Rolls-Royce Pegasus Mk103. Thrust 22,000lb/10,000kg.(UK).

Most common passenger jet engine
Pratt & Whitney JT8D powering Boeing 727, Boeing 737-200, McDonnell Douglas DC-9 etc. Thrust 15,000–20,000lb. Over 13,000 engines produced (USA).

Important dates

120BC   Hero demonstrates principle of jet reaction.

AD1937   World's first turbojet, designed by Frank Whittle (UK), is tested.

1939   First turbojet flight, German Heinkel HE178 (engine was Heinkel HE536).

1941   First British jet engine to power an aircraft, Whittle turbojet Gloster E28139.

1948   First turbojet-powered aircraft to break the sound barrier, de Havilland D.H.108 (UK), powered by de Havilland Ghost turbojet.

1949   First pure jet aircraft into commercial service, de Havilland Comet, powered by Rolls-Royce Avon turbojets (UK).

1955   First use of reheat to increase thrust of a turbojet (UK).

1960   First V/Stol engine tested, Rolls-Royce Pegasus powering P.1127 (UK).

1969   First supersonic passenger aircraft flies – Concorde (UK/France) powered by four Rolls-Royce/Snecma Olympus 593 turbojets, 30,500lb thrust each.

1969   First Boeing 747 Jumbo Jet flies, powered by four high bypass ratio Pratt & Whitney JT9D turbofans, each producing 43,500lbs thrust (USA).

1983   First test of General Electric CF6-80C2 at 62,000lbs thrust – world's most powerful passenger jet engine (USA).

Who makes jet engines?

Programme manager   Every different type of engine manufactured by a company comes under the watchful eye of the programme manager, who makes sure that all aspects of its production and performance go according to plan.

Designers   Responsible for looking after all the different aspects of engine design. The **Chief Designer** is in charge of a team which creates ideas for making and improving every part of a jet engine so that it works as efficiently as possible without being too costly.

Production manager   Heads the team which looks after the building of the engine. He has to ensure that all of the thousands of components are ready at the right time so that the engines are delivered on schedule.

Inspectors   Every stage of engine manufacture has to be checked by qualified inspectors responsible for ensuring that all parts are of the right quality.

Salesmen   Responsible for selling the engine to aircraft manufacturers and airlines.

Engineers   All the different stages of engine manufacture are carried out by highly qualified engineers whose skills range from cutting, shaping and forming, to the testing of parts.

Computer programmers   Modern jet engines are all built with the help of computers, which can simplify many of the manufacturing tasks. Computer programmers write the instructions telling the computers what to do.

Index

Acknowledgements

Threshold Books and the publishers gratefully acknowledge the help given by Rolls-Royce Limited, Derby, in the production of this book.

Illustration credits

Photographs: General Electric, Cincinatti, USA 18 (bottom), 24 (top), 27 (bottom); LAT Photographic 28 (bottom); McDonnell Douglas 28 (top); Pratt & Whitney 10 (bottom), 11, 13 (bottom), 18 (top): Rolls-Royce 2, 4 (bottom), 5, 6, 8, 9, 12 (bottom), 14 (bottom), 15, 16, 19 (bottom), 20 (bottom), 21 (bottom), 22, 23, 25, 26, 27 (top); Turbomeca, Bordes, France 29 (bottom).

Diagrams and drawings: Ray Burrows 3, 4 (top), 5, 7, 10 (top), 12 (top), 14 (top), 17, 18 (top), 19 (top), 20 (top), 21 (top), 24 (bottom), 29 (top); Gillian Newing 13 (top). Diagrams are based on information kindly supplied by Rolls-Royce.

How Jet Engines Are Made
© Threshold Books Limited, 1985
First published in the United States of America by Facts On File, Inc.,
460 Park Avenue South, New York, NY 10016.
First published in Great Britain by Faber and Faber Limited.

General Editor: Barbara Cooper
The How It Is Made series was conceived, designed and produced by Threshold Books Limited,
661 Fulham Road, London SW6.

Library of Congress Cataloging in Publication Data
Moxon, Julian.
  How jet engines are made.
  Summary: Describes how jet engines are made.
  1. Airplanes——Turbojet engines——Juvenile literature.
  [1. Airplanes——Turbojet engines] I. Title.
  TL709.3.T83M65   1985   629.134′353
  84-21049
  ISBN 0-8160-0037-9

Typeset by Phoenix Photosetting, Chatham, Kent, England
Printed and bound in Belgium by Henri Proost & Cie PVBA